what we said

sue chenette
what we said

What We Said

Sue Chenette

© 2019
All Rights Reserved

ISBN 978-1-934894-61-3
POETRY

No portion of this book may be copied, transmitted, duplicated, stored or distributed in any form (including but not limited to print, mechanical, audio, video, digital or electronic means), except for brief excerpts used in reviews or commentaries, without prior express written permission from both the author and the publisher

Front cover design
KEITH KLEESPIES

Book design
EK LARKEN

Published in Kentucky
by

for Jim and Eleanor Bussey
in memory

Introduction

The War on Poverty – does the phrase call up anything for you? I started asking friends, acquaintances, and people met by chance, after a reader wondered who these poems were for – "people who were part of the experiences you write about? I'm thinking that outsiders would need a little more information."

"Some kind of political dog-whistle," answered a baby boomer friend, a woman with a career writing software manuals. A younger woman working three part-time jobs and studying to be a social worker thought of people who can't afford a place to live, "and whole neighborhoods where there's only a corner store and they have to buy expensive junk food." A fellow in his forties, a radiologist and reader of *The New York Times*, mused for a moment. "Whatever war there was on poverty," he said, shaking his head, "has pretty much disintegrated." The woman sitting beside me as we tried on winter boots at SoftMoc was curious about why I'd asked. "Poverty redux," she nodded when I explained. Few remembered LBJ's war in the '60s. Many had not even been born. But their responses made it clear that more than ever, in a society with an increasing gulf between rich and poor, poverty is a pressing problem.

Several people knew that the phrase had originally referred to a specific program launched by Lyndon Johnson in 1964. "Yes, LBJ in the '60s," said a writer friend over lunch. "There was a book, *The Other America*, by Michael Harrington. Kennedy read it and started the program. It was pretty vague. LBJ inherited it and put energy into it."

The War on Poverty was a key constituent in Lyndon Johnson's vision of The Great Society – a vision that would confront poverty, inequality, and racial injustice in America. Legislation was drafted by the President's Task Force under Sargent Shriver, and the Economic Opportunity Act was passed in August 1964. This was the beginning of the Job Corps and Neighborhood Youth Corps, of Adult Basic

Education and community action programs, of Work Study grants, VISTA, and Head Start. To give a helping hand to those most in need was the goal of these programs. The men and women who developed them are described by Michael Gillette in *Launching the War on Poverty, An Oral History*:

> Most of these planners had come of age during the Great Depression and were veterans, in one way or another, of the World War II era. Having conquered two of the twentieth century's greatest challenges, this generation possessed extraordinary self-confidence, determination, and idealism. No task was too formidable. Through vigorous, enlightened government action, society could be improved.

It was a hopeful time, alive with optimism. When the first group of VISTA workers volunteered in December 1964, they came from fifteen states. College-age kids, a nurse, a farmer, teachers and military retirees, their ages ranged from 21 to 71. "We were inexperienced activists filled with the desire to help," a VISTA alum writes, "to do something of value, to make change."

My brother-in-law remembers those years clearly. He grew up in Kentucky, worked as a state trooper before he became a lawyer. "Well, for me it calls up Lyndon Johnson and Bobby Kennedy, Appalachia," he told me. "We were there. I don't think many people have any idea, I don't think they've seen real poverty." He would have been a teenager when Johnson gave his 1964 State of the Union address.

I was a recent college graduate with a degree in music from the University of Wisconsin when I took a job two years later, as a case worker in Knox County, Kentucky.

Many books and articles have debated the ways in which the War on Poverty programs succeeded, and the ways in which they failed. These poems consider my experience, in that particular time and in a particular place.

—Sue Chenette

Barbourville, Kentucky
corner of North Main and Manchester
a short and long block
and part of another
down from Courthouse Square:

KNOX COUNTY DEPARTMENT
OF ECONOMIC SECURITY

Storefront windows
our seven desks

      Ginny's in front of mine

      "Work Experience and Training
      for Unemployed Fathers – but around here
      they call it Happy Pappies," she said
           that fall in 1966
              when I came new to Knox Country
                  following a husband to his teaching job.
"They need case workers."

      Anyone with a degree   My Bachelor of Music
                              and a Civil Service exam

Miz Scelly over-seeing us from the back

                (bent over my typewriter
                fidgeting the file drawer
                musing out the window)

*This administration here and now,
declares unconditional war
on Poverty in America*

*It will not be a short or easy struggle,
no single weapon or strategy will suffice,
but we shall not rest
until that war is won.*

We call it goin' out visiting Miz Scelly said

That first day I went with Ginny
    out 25 E toward Flat Lick
    past Goodin Branch Road
    and the turn to Bimble
    past Turkey Creek and Fortney Branch
    then back in the hills along Stinking Creek
        fenced bottom land
        branching shadow where the road hugged a slope
        now and then a house up close around a curve
        chickens, kids barefoot

A one-day apprenticeship

        How we do the home visit
        its categories including
        the Means Test

Need - Personal Property

The clients state
that they have no
checking account
savings account
insurance
stocks
bonds
certificates of deposit
postal savings
or
prepaid burial

Since this has been
previously verified
local and county records
were not checked
at this time.

After, I drove the county roads alone

    in the hollers

        in fall

        pale leaves of burley
        curing in the open barns

        stooked hay where the land
        sloped steeply up

        cows along the creek

*Dominantly Steep and Very Steep,
Well Drained and Moderately Well Drained,
Deep and Moderately Deep Soils, on Uplands*

>*Most of the acreage
is used as woodland,
but a small acreage, primarily
in narrow valleys, is used
for pasture and crops.*
>
>*Steepness of slope on the uplands
and the hazard of
flooding in the narrow valleys
are the main
limitations
for most uses.*

in the hills

      buckeye
      hickory
      white oak
      red oak
      tulip poplar
      beech
      chestnut

            second and third growth

The Trees in 1870

*For and in consideration of
the sum of $20,000,
the grantor hereby
bargains,
sells,
grants
and conveys unto the grantee
40,000
poplar and
whiteoak trees, each
of said trees to measure
not less than 30 inches
in diameter under the bark,
stump high, measuring
three feet above the ground,
without fire damage or
blemish; and
the grantee shall have
two years after the date hereof
to mark said trees
with his brand.*

Men brought their wives along:
We heard
about this Happy Pappy program.

*

Precipitating problem

The client has been unable
to find work since
the C&H Mine shut down.

Clarification of policy

CW explained that the program
provides a supportive need-based grant
for 3 years of training after which
the participant is expected
to find regular employment

1888

*Things changed in 1888,
when the Cumberland Valley Branch
of the Louisville & Nashville Railway
was built through the county*

*In 1888, a coal company began mining
on a considerable scale. Mining
became the chief occupation of the people.
There was no part of Knox County
in which coal was not found in large deposits.*

coal smoke and rooster cries
    cold packed earth on the walk from the car
      Instant Maxwell House, very strong,
        the best chair offered
          the ritual of the visit
            a kind of work we did together

        almost a dance

    (questions + appropriate answers = monthly check)

Home management

The clients stated
that they put up
new sheetrock
in the bedroom and
have purchased
a washing machine
on installments.

(and who was I to say

    beans and flour in bulk
      no more Moon Pies
        to speak of housekeeping
          to women who swept their floors
            clean of cannel coal dust
              from the grate each day?

                  I didn't.)

Home Environment - Neighborhood

The family home is located
on the main road through
this part of the county,
the Hinkle-Girdler loop.
There are many homes
along the black-top road and
in the hollows branching off.

Girdler School is two miles
in one direction, and Grove Center
one-half mile in the other.
Both Girdler Holiness Church
and Callebs Creek Baptist
are easily accessible.

All of the community resources
of Barbourville, 10 miles distant,
are readily available
due to good roads and
the family's ownership of a car.

The family is happy
with their surroundings.
CW concurs that this
is a desirable place to live.

Poem in which I try to imagine moments I couldn't know
after photographs by John Dominis

    rush-seat chair
    sit a moment now
    daughter heavy-limp
    sick with measles
    asleep in her lap
    barefoot
    outgrew those shoes

          *

    pretty leaves on these plates

    over to Barbourville they come free
    at the grocery

    not a whole set

    corn bread turned out good
    more soup beans next time in town

    that lil gal from the welfare
    says get them eating greens

          *

long johns half-froze on the line
wash day's wash day
hauling water

real pretty in the woods though
bush like a meringue pie

Frankie down by the tracks
looking for chunk coal fell off the train

*

"Hold still, so I can get your ears.
We'll get Sissy to pour in more hot
afterwards, and I'll squeeze
the flannel over your shoulder."

Pokey shoulder blade,
and his skin so soft.

driving back

    along Paynes Branch
        Hawn Branch
        Valentine

    I might meet a work crew

        mud roads
        chug holes
        pick-up truck

    men hauling stones from scrubby hillsides
    filling in ruts and gouges

Work Experience and Training

The project supervisor reports
that the client is assigned to
one of the work crews
rocking the county roads

an activity
of use to the community
while serving to develop
proper work habits
and attitudes.

In winter the shapes of hills showed
    snow-curved among stiff straight trees

      a trick I learned on the rutted roads
        loose grip on the wheel
           let the car ('51 Chevy, bad shocks) lurch
          and right itself as it would

*The topography is a series of mountain ridges winding in all sorts of fantastic curves, separated by long, narrow and winding creek valleys.
More than three-fourths of the territory is steep mountain sides.*

That little brown-headed gal, she sure can drive
Bobby Longsworth said to Randy the Project Supervisor
who, laughing, reported it back to me, pretty much
the way it happened
that day I drove up the hill to Roy Mills' place
just off the Hinkle-Girdler road
valley dropping vertical on my right
trees and boulders steep above on the left.
Leaving I thought I'd do a Y turn
the way I used to on county roads in Wisconsin
and I backed around
rear bumper butted up against the rocky rise
front wheels hanging over bottom land
Bobby Longsworth just coming out from Payne's store
saw my car dangling, drove on up the hill
nosed his long blue Ford close
to my green Chevrolet.
They worked deliberately, he and Mr. Mills,
not fast or slow not saying much
jacking up the front end of my car
chaining the two front ends together.
Then Bobby Longsworth got in his car
backed up fast, pulling
my Chevy off the jack, yanking it around.

`They poured a bucket of water in the radiator.

How my mother remembers it

Oh, that was the time when those men just
picked your car up and turned it around.
I can see them there, sitting under that big tree.
And they didn't have very much to do, because
there wasn't very much for them to do there, so
they were just kind of lazing around. In the shade.
But they were very helpful. They came over and
lifted it right up and set it down the other way
so you could get on with where you had to go.

School Attendance

CW verified
that Darla age 7
and Sonny age 9
attend Girdler School

Laura Mae age 16
has re-enrolled
at Knox Central

The family was informed
that their grant will be
increased accordingly,
the Title V act stipulating
that the allotment for
each school-age child
will be awarded only
if that child is
in regular school
attendance.

What we said

At least the kids will have a better chance

You won't want to go up that holler till the rains let up
    Miz Scelly advised in March
       The ford'll be flooded too deep to cross

So that was an office day for sure

coffee break with Ginny at Foley's just around the corner
Ken and Randy playing the pinball machines in back

     Ka-chup whrmm Bp bp bp bp Ka-chupka-
         chupka-chup rhmmm
            clp

glazed donuts grilled in butter
    (two)
        (squished down caramelized)

   Foley in his red apron: They say
that weather's comin' up through the gap

In Cumberland gap
it got so cold
I couldn't keep from freezin' to death
to save my soul

What Bobby Longsworth asked Randy

They're not goin' to take me off this program, are they?

*The heavy dependence
on the coal industry
in Kentucky coal producing counties
often leaves these counties
susceptible to changes in
the fortunes of the industry.*

*As a result, losses
in coal mining earnings
in these counties often
leads to increased poverty
and dependence
on social welfare programs.*

Late April, and the earth warming

    redbud and dogwood

        hollers greening

            a man and a plow mule

                furrows shining

*Before the railroad came
the majority of the county's vast
resources were for home
use and local trade.*

*Corn, wheat, oats,
and tobacco were
the chief crops grown.*

*Potatoes, turnips, cabbages, and
all kinds of garden vegetables
gave excellent yields.*

*Apples, peaches, pears, cherries, plums,
and all the varieties of
smaller fruits, berries, and nuts
scarcely ever fail of a full crop.*

I drove up Callebs Creek, to see Ralph Calleb

>They took me off rockin' the roads, he said
>give me a job at Knox County General Supply.
>
>That's wonderful, Mr. Calleb.
>Randy says they're training you to be a clerk.
>
>Well, they got me in the box room
>that's the job they give me for now.

He had made me a gift

>three picture frames
>old chestnut – worm-stippled wood
>
>They are made with skill
>the inner edges smoothly beveled

Potential for employment

The client is
hard-working
and adaptable.
His situation
is limited
by the lack
of jobs
in Knox County.

*The training myth ...
kept Americans from thinking
about the limits
of a capitalist boom
as an antipoverty weapon,
for they focused on
defects in the worker rather
than those
in the labor markets.*

Postscript

Decades after I left the job for graduate school in music, and long, too, after the Reagan administration repealed the Economic Opportunity Act, I drove through Barbourville on my way somewhere else. I thought, coffee at Foley's, but it was boarded up. On the Hinkle-Girdler loop, new brick homes sat back from the road on mowed lawns. The creek bottoms where tobacco and corn had grown were back to brush. New prosperity: coal booming again, with mountain-top removal, and a market for timber. And – or so the rumor went – marijuana crops tended by Vietnam vets. A shopping mall out on the highway, the blocks around the Courthouse Square half-razed for parking lots.

I wanted to find a stone schoolhouse I'd seen once in a snow storm. I had to drive the loop twice, stopping, the second time, to ask at the Quick Mart. Hey Lester, the counter guy called to someone in back, Didn't there use to be a school up Callebs Creek? Didn't your brother go up there?

I'd driven past. It was a house now. The same stones, though, as that November afternoon –

fat wet flakes, spinning —
first snow. In the schoolyard
children ran and shouted,
chasing each other in circles.

On down the holler, along the gravel road
cattle bunched close to the fence,
rubbing together as the snow fell and melted
on their warm heads and backs.

Notes and Acknowledgements

The found poems in italics are quoted or condensed from the following sources:

This administration here and now
Lyndon Johnson, 1964 State of the Union Address

Dominantly Steep and Very Steep
Soil Survey of Knox County and Eastern Part of Whitley County, Kentucky. US Department of Agriculture, 1988.

The Trees in 1870
a timber deed quoted by Henry Caudill in *Night Comes to the Cumberlands*. 1962. Ashland, Kentucky: Jesse Stuart Foundation, 2001.

1888
Secrist, M. *Knox County, Kentucky History Through Biographical and Genealogical Sketches of Its Ancestors*. M. Secrist, 2012.

The topography is a series
Ibid.

In Cumberland gap
Appalachian folk song quoted by Henry Caudill in *Night Comes to the Cumberlands*.

The heavy dependence
Roenker, Jonathan M. "The Economic Impact of Coal in Appalachian Kentucky." This article is based on and draws from the 2001 University of Kentucky Center for Business and Economic Research publication "A Study on the Current Economic Impacts of the Appalachian Coal Industry and its Future in the Region."

Before the railroad came
Secrist, M.

The training myth
>Stricker, Frank. *Why America Lost the War on Poverty – and How to Win It*. Chapel Hill: The University of North Carolina Press, 2007.

The John Dominis photos were taken in 1964 and can be seen online at https://www.vintag.es/2018/04/appalachians-life-1964.html.

Michael L. Gillette's *Launching the War on Poverty, An Oral History* (Oxford University Press, 2010) was an important reference when writing the introduction to these poems. I am also indebted to the website VISTA TIMELINE – Celebrating 50 Years of VISTA Service, and to VISTA Campus, where I found memories from VISTA alumni.

The first draft of *What We Said* was written in a workshop led by Hoa Nguyen and devoted to reading aloud, and writing under the influence of, *The Maximus Poems* of Charles Olson. I am grateful to Hoa and to the poets who shared those afternoons.

Many thanks to Maureen Hynes for her insightful reading of an early version of the manuscript. Thanks, too, to Frank Stricker for asking the right questions, and to Peter Sanders, Maureen Hynes, and Ruth Roach Pierson for thoughtful readings of the introduction.

For friendship, fellowship, and inspired suggestions, thanks to members of the Weeping Purple Beech poetry group and the U of T Victoria University group.

To Scout Larken, guiding spirit and publisher of MotesBooks, thanks for belief in the poems, and for skill in all things typographical.

To Keith Kleespies, many thanks for the evocative cover.

To my sister Liz Fentress, more thanks than I can express for generous enthusiasm and help in making this book a reality.

And as ever, I am deeply grateful to my husband Steve for his unfailing support and encouragement.

ABOUT THE AUTHOR

Sue Chenette is the author of *Slender Human Weight* (Guernica Editions, 2009) and *The Bones of His Being* (Guernica Editions, 2012) as well as three chapbooks: *Solitude in Cloud and Sun*, *A Transport of Grief*, and *The Time Between Us*. A classical pianist, poet, and editor, she grew up in northern Wisconsin and has made her home in Toronto since 1972.

www.ingramcontent.com/pod-product-compliance
Lightning Source LLC
Chambersburg PA
CBHW032104040426
42449CB00007B/1176